Date: 11/17/22

**3650 Summit Boulevard
West Palm Beach, FL 33406**

Cultural Cuisine

EMPANADAS

by Richard Sebra

abdobooks.com

Published by Pop!, a division of ABDO, PO Box 398166,
Minneapolis, Minnesota 55439. Copyright ©2021 by POP, LLC.
International copyrights reserved in all countries. No part
of this book may be reproduced in any form without written
permission from the publisher. Pop!™ is a trademark and logo
of POP, LLC.

Printed in the United States of America, North Mankato,
Minnesota

082020
012021

THIS BOOK CONTAINS
RECYCLED MATERIALS

Cover Photo: Shutterstock Images
Interior Photos: Shutterstock Images, 1, 9, 11, 10, 13, 14–15, 17, 20, 21
(left), 21 (middle), 26, 27, 28, 29; iStockphoto, 5, 7, 6, 21 (right), 22,
25; Nora Yusuf/Alamy, 12; Ildi.Food/Alamy, 18–19

Editor: Sophie Geister-Jones
Series Designers: Candice Keimig, Victoria Bates, and Laura
Graphenteen

Library of Congress Control Number: 2019954987
Publisher's Cataloging-in-Publication Data
Names: Sebra, Richard, author.
Title: Empanadas / by Richard Sebra
Description: Minneapolis, Minnesota : POP!, 2021 | Series:
    Cultural cuisine | Includes online resources and index.
Identifiers: ISBN 9781532167744 (lib. bdg.) | ISBN 9781532168840
    (ebook)
Subjects: LCSH: Empanadas--Juvenile literature. | Turnovers
    (Cooking)--Juvenile literature. | Ethnic food--Juvenile
    literature. | International cooking--Juvenile literature. |
    Food--Social aspects--Juvenile literature.
Classification: DDC 641.598--dc23

WELCOME TO DiscoverRoo!

Pop open this book and you'll find QR codes loaded

with information, so you can learn even more!

Scan this code* and others like
it while you read, or visit the
website below to make this
book pop!

popbooksonline.com/empanadas

*Scanning QR codes requires a web-enabled smart device with a QR code reader app and a camera.

TABLE OF
CONTENTS

CHAPTER 1

ALL WRAPPED UP

Empanada stands line the busy streets. Each stand sells trays of golden-brown **pastries**. A customer selects one and takes a bite. Steam rushes out of the hot crust. Delicious meat and cheese are packed inside.

WATCH A VIDEO HERE!

Empanadas are often filled with ground meat, such as beef.

People often buy empanadas from food trucks.

An empanada is a pocket of **dough** containing a filling. This filling often has meat and vegetables.

Empanadas are a popular street food in Latin America. Their small size makes them easy to carry and eat. They're a great choice for a quick, tasty lunch.

DID YOU KNOW?

Empanada is pronounced em-puh-NAH-duh.

CHAPTER 2

SPAIN TO SOUTH AMERICA

Empanadas can be found all over the world. They are especially popular in South America. People in Argentina have been making empanadas for hundreds of years. But the food got its start in Europe.

COMPLETE AN ACTIVITY HERE!

Cooks fold empanadas in different shapes depending on what country they are from.

People in northern Spain still make large, pie-like empanadas today.

The first empanadas were made in northern Spain. Recipes from there began to appear in the 1500s. However, these early empanadas were larger.

They were not folded into small pockets.

Instead, they were more like pies. People

would cut them into slices.

In Peru, people often bake empanadas in stone ovens.

Throughout the 1500s, Spanish

immigrants brought the dish to South

America. In South America, empanadas

got smaller and became a handheld

food. People began making individual

pastries. People considered them the

perfect meal to eat while working.

Miners and farmers would bring empanadas for lunch. They were easy to eat during the workday.

At first, people filled empanadas with meat. They often used ox meat or pork. Later, people began trying new flavors. They added vegetables, eggs, cheese, and other **ingredients**. Today, there are many types of empanadas. Meat remains a common filling. Other empanadas hold fruit or vegetables instead. There are even dessert empanadas.

Some dessert empanadas are filled with a creamy chocolate.

CHAPTER 3

IN THE KITCHEN

Making empanadas starts with the **dough**. The dough is made from water, butter, flour, and salt. It also includes a **spice** called paprika. The cook mixes all

TRY A RECIPE HERE!

Cooks only knead empanada dough a little. That keeps the dough smooth and stretchy.

these **ingredients** together. Then the

dough must chill in the refrigerator.

While the dough chills, the cook makes the filling. First, the cook browns the meat in a pan. Then the cook mixes in vegetables, onions, and other ingredients. Finally, the cook adds spices

Empanadas from Argentina traditionally hold ground beef, olives, raisins, and hard-boiled eggs.

to the filling. Spices, such as cumin and paprika, add even more flavor.

The cook rolls balls of dough into flat circles. A spoonful of filling goes in the center of each circle.

Some people crimp the empanadas' edges with their hands. Others use a fork instead.

The cook folds the dough over the filling. Then the cook **crimps** the edges. This step seals the filling inside.

The empanadas are now ready to cook. They can be fried or baked. The dough becomes crisp and flaky.

THE PERFECT FOLD

Each empanada must be folded carefully. The cook makes sure the edges line up. Then the cook presses them together. A cook can use several different folds.

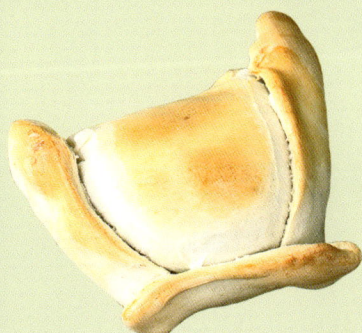

Spanish Empanada

Chilean Empanada

Argentine Empanada

DID YOU KNOW? The name *empanada* comes from the Spanish word *empanar*. It means "to wrap something in bread."

RECIPE CHECKLIST

DOUGH INGREDIENTS

◇ 1 cup water

◇ 3/4 cup butter

◇ 2 3/4 cups flour

◇ 2 teaspoons salt

◇ 1 teaspoon paprika

FILLING INGREDIENTS

◇ 1 pound ground meat

◇ 1/2 cup chopped green onions

◇ 1 cup chopped olives

◇ 1 teaspoon salt

◇ 1/2 teaspoon paprika

◇ 1/2 teaspoon garlic powder

Makes 12 empanadas

INSTRUCTIONS

Dough:

1. Heat the butter and water until the butter is melted.
2. In a separate bowl, combine all dough ingredients and mix together.
3. Chill the dough in the refrigerator.
4. Remove dough from fridge and separate into small balls.
5. Roll balls of dough into thin circles.

Filling:

6. Cook the meat.
7. Stir in the other ingredients.
8. Scoop filling onto one circle of dough.
9. Fold the dough over the filling.
10. Crimp the edges closed.
11. Bake or fry the empanadas.

CHAPTER 4

A FESTIVE FOOD

Empanadas can be a meal, a snack, or

a dessert. Because of their small size,

empanadas make a great party food.

They can be made in large **batches**.

And they are easy to eat while walking.

LEARN MORE HERE!

Fruit fillings are popular for dessert empanadas.

Some empanadas are filled with sausage or asparagus.

The **pastries** are a common part of celebrations in Argentina. Different parts of the country have their own versions of empanadas. They are cooked and filled in different ways.

FANCY FILLINGS

An empanada's filling changes depending on where it comes from. In Buenos Aires, people fill them with meat and cheese. In Jujuy, they use goat meat. In Cordoba, people make sweet empanadas. They have sugar, beef, raisins, and potatoes. Other empanadas are filled with sweet squash. These sweet empanadas are dusted with sugar.

An empanada can be folded differently based on what its filling is.

Some people make new empanada filling flavors, such as pizza.

Empanadas have also spread

around the world. Every place puts its

own twist on the food. In each country,

people use **ingredients** common in that

part of the world.

MAKING CONNECTIONS

TEXT-TO-SELF

Would you rather eat a dessert empanada or a

traditional empanada? Why?

TEXT-TO-TEXT

Have you read books about other foods that

are fried? How are those foods similar to

empanadas? How are they different?

TEXT-TO-WORLD

Why do you think empanadas in different parts

of the world have different ingredients?

GLOSSARY

batch — a group of things made at one time.

crimp — to pinch or press together in order to seal.

dough — mixture of moist flour that is thick enough to roll.

immigrant — a person who moves from one country to another country.

ingredient — one substance used in a mixture.

pastry — a baked food item with a high fat content.

spice — an ingredient used to add flavor to food.

INDEX

ONLINE RESOURCES
popbooksonline.com

Scan this code* and others like it while you read, or visit the website below to make this book pop!

popbooksonline.com/empanadas

*Scanning QR codes requires a web-enabled smart device with a QR code reader app and a camera.